I0774513

Welcome to the Enchanting World of "100 MANDALAS FOR CALMNESS" Coloring Book for Adults!

Step into a world of tranquility and creativity with our meticulously curated collection of 100 mandalas designed to bring a sense of serenity to your coloring experience. Each mandala is a journey in mindfulness, a canvas waiting for your artistic touch to unfold. Let the harmonious patterns guide you as you embark on a therapeutic adventure of coloring and self-discovery.

Happy coloring!

Thank you for allowing our book to be a part of your journey to inner peace and tranquil. As I express my heartfelt gratitude for choosing our Mandala coloring book, we genuinely hope that it was relaxing and enjoyable coloring it bringing you endless hours of calm and meditation.

Your support for our creativity will significantly motivates us to craft quality products that bring added value to your life.

If you have any suggestions or feedback, please feel free to drop us a line at joanaseabeam@gmail.com We're always keen to hear from our valued customers.

If you liked our coloring book, we'd be immensely encouraged by your review on the Amazon page. It helps us grow and serve you better.

Please use the code to Navigate there

You may also like to check our other books

Again, our deepest gratitude for your continued support